Go(o)d for You:

The Divine Code of 7 Noahide Commandments

Third Edition

Contributors:

Rabbi Moshe Weiner

Rabbi J. Immanuel Schochet, Ph.D

Rabbi Shimon D. Cowen, Ph.D

Michael Schulman, Ph.D (Editor)

Joseph M. Regenstein, Ph.D

Arthur Goldberg, J.D.

Published by
Ask Noah International

Go(o)d for You: The Divine Code of 7 Noahide Commandments

ISBN 978-1-7323735-7-0 (3rd Edition)
Published by
Ask Noah International Inc.
P.O. Box 1
Pittsburgh, PA 15230-0001 USA
Email: SevenLaws@asknoah.org
Web: https://asknoah.org

Graphic design by Brandyn Ashing

Please preserve the sanctity of this booklet.

Table of Contents

Starting from a Moral Code that Unites All Mankind   2

Seven Commandments: An Introduction   5

1. The Prohibition of Idolatry   7

2. The Prohibition of Blasphemy   10

3. The Prohibition of Murder and Injury   13

4. The Prohibition of Eating Meat that was Removed from a Living Animal   17

5. The Prohibition of Theft   21

6. The Prohibition of Forbidden Sexual Relations   24

7. The Obligation for Laws and Courts   28

What other righteous traditions were accepted by mankind after the Flood?   31

Our opportunity to all be on the same page   36

Starting from a Moral Code that Unites All Mankind

"Message from the Rebbe," reprinted from
Lubavitch International, **vol. 2, no. 1, 1990**

We find ourselves now at a turning point in history. Changes have swept the world as dissolving repressive regimes have given way to a climate of increased moral consciousness. It is thus an appropriate time to reflect upon the dynamics of these changes and thereby draw encouragement and guidance to affect them fully. In explaining the purpose of Creation, our sages say that G-d, the Essence of all good, created the world as a result of His desire to do good. As it says in Psalms 145, "The L-rd is good to all, and His mercies are over all His works." For as it is the nature of good to do good unto others, the creation of the universe was a Divine expression of goodness. In this way, the universe and all life are recipients and objects of Divine goodness.

Hence, everything that occurs in the world, even the apparent bad, such as natural disasters, must ultimately have redeeming good. Similarly, the negative inclination within human beings, who essentially desire to do good, is but a "mechanism" by G-d's design to establish free choice. For had G-d created a world that is totally and exclusively good, without any efforts on the part of mankind to achieve it, there would be no or little appreciation of goodness. In light of this, it is important to realize that in the individual's struggle with evil, within the world at large or within one's self, the approach should not be one of confrontation. *Rather, by emphasizing that which is good in people and in the world, and by bringing the positive to the fore, the evil is superseded by the good, until it eventually disappears.*

Although G-d created the world giving people free choice, He nevertheless has given us the tools and the guidance we need to encourage us to choose the good:

a Divine moral code, one that predates all human codes, and the only one that has timeless and universal application for a good, moral civilization. This Divine code, known as the Seven Laws of Noah, establishes an objective definition of "good" – one that applies to all people. For as recent history has proven, a morality that is based on human ideas of good is relative, subjective, and essentially not persuasive. Furthermore, as is abundantly clear to educators and law-enforcement agents, neither intimidation nor threat of punishment can foster a deep sense of moral obligation. This can only come from the knowledge – through education, that there is an "Eye that sees and an Ear that hears" to Whom we are all accountable.

The Noahide Code of seven basic Divine laws was given to Noah and his children after the Flood. These laws would assure Noah and his children, the forebears of the new human race, that humanity would not degenerate into a jungle again. *The laws, which command the establishment of courts of justice and prohibit idolatry, blasphemy, homicide, incest, robbery, and eating flesh of a live animal (cruelty to animals), are the foundation of all morality. And they extend, by laws derived from these, into all aspects of moral behavior.*

A particular task is to educate and to encourage the observance of the Seven Laws among all people. The religious tolerance of today and the trend towards greater freedom gives us the unique opportunity to enhance widespread observance of these laws. For it is by adherence to these laws, which are in and of themselves an expression of Divine goodness, that all humankind is united and bound by a common moral responsibility to our Creator. This unity promotes peace and harmony among all people, thereby achieving the ultimate good. As the Psalmist said in Psalms 133: "How good and how pleasant it is for brothers to dwell together in unity."

From a 1990 address by

the Lubavitcher Rebbe,

Rabbi Menachem Mendel Schneerson

© by Linda Frimer

4

Seven Commandments:
An Introduction

After the Flood, G-d established the Covenant of the Rainbow with Noah and all of the world's creatures. This covenant is not dependent on mankind's observance of the Seven Laws of Noah. Rather, the Noahide Code established the context *and the eventual goal* for a renewed world in which this covenant could be the open and enduring expression of G-d's love for His creation. It was G-d's promise to all living creatures that He would never again obliterate all land-life from the world, as stated in Genesis 9:11 – "never again will there be a flood to destroy the earth." *The Covenant of the Rainbow has an inner meaning as well: it was G-d's promise that He would always accept a person's sincere personal repentance if it was directed to Him.* From that point on, G-d endowed mankind with the ability to seek and gain His forgiveness, and with this He insured that a person's freedom to choose good includes the strength to prevail over animalistic and self-centered desires.

Still, the Seven Laws received by Noah could have been challenged at a later time by any charismatic misleader who also claimed to be a prophet, and how would a person know which course to follow? This points to the singular importance of the revelation at Mount Sinai to the Jewish people, 50 days after G-d brought them out from slavery in Egypt. At Mount Sinai, the Creator revealed Himself to a nation of at least three million people, making them all witnesses to testify to their future children and the world, so that no person in any generation could arise to seriously refute the prophecy and instruction which Moses received, which is called the Torah. Included in the Torah was the Noahide Code, to be preserved for the generations of mankind.

The entire Book of Genesis, and the Book of Exodus up to and including the arrival of the Israelites at Mount Sinai, were dictated by G-d to Moses when they arrived there. There was then a first covenant made between G-d and the Israelites on that first part of the Written Torah, which included their acceptance of the Noahide Code. Thus, the universal Divine moral code of seven commandments was renewed, after it had become neglected by the nations. That was four days before the Ten Commandments were spoken openly by G-d to all of the Israelites, at which point they became the Jewish people.

At Mount Sinai, G-d taught the essentials of the Torah's precepts through Moses, and this is called the Oral Torah. Included in this are the details of G-d's directive for all Gentiles to observe their Seven Noahide Commandments. These details, as G-d specified them to Moses, are the true foundation of the universal Noahide Code. A righteous Gentile merits to receive a place in the eternal future World to Come, in the Messianic Era, through observance of these commandments. That is a Gentile's part in the Torah of Moses, which is G-d's "Tree of Life" (Proverbs 3:18).

It all begins with recognizing the perfect Unity of the Creator.

1. The Prohibition of Idolatry

Directing our Spirituality to the Creator

The Meaning

The prohibition of idolatry, and its positive aspect of belief in G-d, are the foundation of the Noahide Code. It is the concept that every person is responsible to the One True G-d, regardless of the society's norms and one's own preferences. It is the knowledge that all people are under the One G-d as the Supreme Authority and the ultimate Source of all blessings, and that any other entity (real or imagined) which a person serves and worships as an independent power has become that person's idol.

"The foundation of all foundations and the pillar of wisdom is to know that there is a Primary Being who brought into being all existence. Everything came into existence only from the truth of His being."

— Opening words of *Mishneh Torah* by Rabbi Moshe ben Maimon (Maimonides)

From the Introduction by Rabbi J. Immanuel Schochet to the section on the Prohibition of Idolatry, in "The Divine Code," Part II:

The prohibition of idolatry includes any assumptions of there being self-contained beings or forces that are not totally dependent on G-d and His Providence. This will be understood with the following example: when driving in a nail with a hammer, the immediate agent of activity seems to be the hammer. In truth, however, it is not the hammer itself, but the hand that holds it and the energy used by the hand. So, too, everything in the physical universe and the spiritual realms is forever altogether subject to G-d and His will.

It is forbidden to put one's faith into a belief that planets or constellations *determine* human events or a person's fate. Likewise, soothsaying is a custom that comes from idolatry, and it is forbidden to pick natural occurrences or random lots as signs for how one should choose to act (for example, if a bird tapped on the window, or based on rolling dice, or dealing from a deck of cards). It is forbidden to engage in any form of sorcery (thinking that thereby one can manipulate future events), or to consult "spirits" (as people do in séances). Necromancy and other forms of divination are in the same category. All these practices imply a belief that there are various powers in existence which work on their own, independent of the continuous unified Divine Providence governing the totality of creation.

Human frailty is centered on self-interest, self-indulgence, and gratification: the egocentric as opposed to the theocentric. The powerful desire to control, direct, and manipulate the unknown future, to circumvent the Divine "system," is extremely seductive. In effect however, it betrays a lack of trust in G-d and undermines true belief in G-d, Who alone is the Creator and Sustainer of all beings, and Who alone is in exclusive charge of all that happens to them. Idolatry is thus denial of pure monotheism, and it presupposes a polytheistic—or at least a dualistic—reality. Even if a person chooses to believe in only one idol, the person has set up for himself two deities—his idol, and himself as the appointer of the idol.

The Noahide Code was given by G-d at Mount Sinai, and it serves as the antidote to avoid idolatry's pitfalls, to guide a person in the path of authentic truth, and to help us live up to the fact that every person is created in the "image of G-d."

Scriptural Sources

Genesis 2:16 states: "And the L-rd G-d (*E-lokim*) commanded the man, saying..." The singular Hebrew word *E-lokim* is one of the Divine Names for the One G-d. But the same word is used in the non-holy plural sense to refer to physical or conceptual idolatries (other "gods"), as in the verse, "You shall have no other gods before Me" (Exodus 20:3). Thus the statement in Genesis 2:16 implies that only the L-rd G-d – the One Who commands mankind – should be served and worshiped, but not an idol.

The Hebrew Bible is filled with statements from G-d to His prophets about His abhorrence of all types of idolatry, and His desire that all people shall repent from idolatry and accept Him as their G-d.

Some Details and Related Principles

- The obligation to recognize and believe in the One G-d.

- The obligation for a person to obey what he is commanded by G-d.

- The obligation for a person to pray to G-d. (At the very least, this applies in times of need.)

- The prohibition of serving idols, either instead of or in combination with G-d.

- The prohibition of making, owning, or selling an idol.

- The prohibition of swearing in a name of an idol.

- The prohibition of following the idolatrous customs of those who serve idols. Soothsaying, divination, sorcery and necromancy are included in this prohibition.

2. The Prohibition of Blasphemy

Respecting the Creator

The Meaning

At the most basic level, this means that one must not curse the Creator as He is known by His holy Names. Humans are graced with a unique faculty of speech, which is drawn down from the reflection of Divinity that is uniquely bestowed upon a human being. What greater misuse of this gift could there be than to acknowledge the existence of the Creator, while in the same breath expressing a base and vengeful desire that He should be harmed. It would show that the person does not merely lack faith and trust in the intrinsic good of Divine Providence (which may be hidden for a period of time), but he openly rebels against it.

The following is adapted from the Introduction by Rabbi J. Immanuel Schochet to the Prohibition of Blasphemy, in "The Divine Code," Part III:

At the very center of this world are *homo sapiens*, humans Divinely endowed with intellect. This allows us analytical thought and examination of ourselves and the world around us. Without Divinely-endowed criteria for truth and moral values, however, our critical thinking is abstract and theoretical at best, and obviously susceptible to error.

Thus G-d revealed to mankind knowledge of His inscrutable Will by means of His prophets and the Torah, to know what is right and what is wrong, what is good and what is evil.

The Divine revelation of the Torah at Mount Sinai, and the Divine designation of Moses as the foremost prophet for all time, set forth the ultimate test for the truth of future prophets, i.e., compatibility with the Torah and its eternal commandments. Even so, this legal and moral code is meaningful only when applying the other special gift endowed upon humans, namely freedom of choice to follow or reject proper conduct.

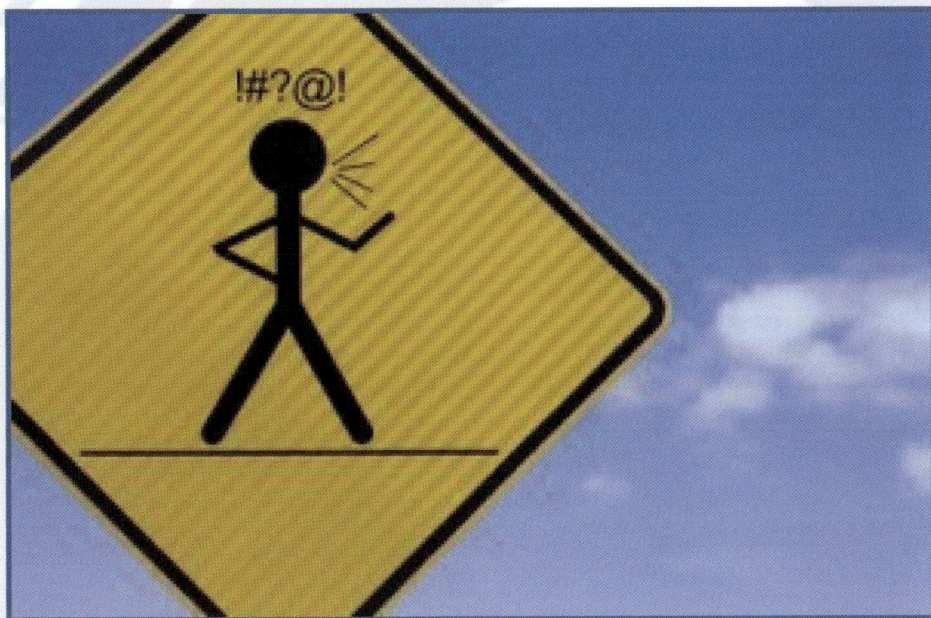

Open-minded and consistent reasoning readily leads to a realization that there must be a Supreme Cause for our most complex yet intricately precise world. Thus we arrive at the recognition and acknowledgment of G-d as Creator, Sovereign and Sustainer of the universe. This is not only an intellectual conclusion, but of itself has practical implications. Noting that life, health, and all human needs and blessings emanate unceasingly from the Creator, we must surely acknowledge this in thought, speech, and action. We ought to express gratitude for the Divine benevolence on which we are continuously dependent, and make ourselves into worthy recipients thereof. This is the concept of worshiping G-d that applies equally to all people alike.

The diametric opposite to this ideal of reverence for G-d is the crass and sinful conduct of deprecating G-d or His Sovereignty. This is referred to as blasphemy. In common usage, the word "blasphemy" is generally defined as any form of uttered impiety, irreverence, or sacrilege against G-d. These are acts of defiance seeking to impair the appropriate respect and reverence for G-d.

More specifically, the prohibition of blasphemy against the blessed Name of the Creator, and the obligation to respect and revere Him, derive from His absolute supremacy and sovereignty. It then follows that:

- Everyone is subject to the precept of awe and reverence before G-d, commonly referred to as the "fear of G-d."

- One may not use G-d's Name in vain. Using G-d's Name in vain is closely connected with the principle of blasphemy, and it is clearly a form of disrespect. Included in this is a prohibition against swearing to a lie in G-d's Name. Thus we find that from the earliest times, the concept of an oath was regarded as a sacred obligation. (See Genesis 21:22 and following, and Genesis 26:28 and following)

Scriptural Sources

Leviticus 24:10-17 relates the incident of a Jew who violated the injunction of Exodus 22:27 and blasphemed in anger, and the Divine edict proclaiming this to be a capital offense. Moreover, it states in Leviticus 24:15, *"ish ish* (any man) who curses his G-d shall bear his sin."* Why the double expression of *"ish ish"* (literally: a man, a man)? To include all mankind.

Some Details and Related Principles

- The obligation to respect G-d's Name.

- The obligation to fear G-d.

- The prohibition of cursing G-d (Heaven forbid).

- The prohibition of swearing in vain (as in taking a vain oath, or swearing to a false promise or statement).

- Which vows may be annulled, and the justifications and methods for doing so.

3. The Prohibition of Murder and Injury
Guarding the Sanctity of Human Life

> Rabbi Akiva said: "Beloved is humankind, for they were created in the image of the Creator; it is an even greater love that it was made known to them that they were created in the image of the Creator, as it is stated [Genesis 9:6]: For He made humankind in the Divine image."
>
> —Ethics of the Fathers, Ch 3.

The Meaning
The following is adapted from the Introduction by Dr. Michael Schulman to the section on the Prohibition of Murder and Injury, in "The Divine Code," Part V:

Human life is an unalienable right of every person, and a gift from G-d that He expects us to guard and respect. Mankind was created "in the image of G-d," and therefore possesses a dimension of holiness. Taking a human life diminishes a measure of the Divine image that is present in the world, and without G-d's permission it is strictly forbidden. Furthermore, murder is an act of extreme rebellion against G-d Himself, Who blessed mankind "to be fruitful and multiply and fill the earth" (Genesis 1:28), and "He did not create it for emptiness; He fashioned it to be inhabited" (Isaiah 45:18).

In addition, a person who murders harms many others as well. The tragic loss of a person's life afflicts his loved ones, his friends, and his associates. The effects of murder also extend across time and space. A murderer also "kills" his victim's would-be descendants for all generations to come. All that potential for good throughout the future has been lost because of the violent act. Even if the victim would not have subsequently had any children, all of a person's great or small good deeds are the spiritual fruits that he adds to the world. Therefore, the Jewish Sages taught that someone who causes the destruction of one person's life from the world is considered as if he destroyed an entire world, and conversely, someone who saves or sustains one person's life in the world is considered as if he saved an entire world.

Yet what acts constitute the sin of murder? Are there times when killing is permitted by the Torah? Does a person ever have the "right" to end his or her own life? What about engaging in activities that are inherently life threatening, or accepting donor organs from living persons who will not regain consciousness? In the Noahide Code, G-d provided ample instructions for how the commandment applies in any circumstance.

Furthermore, the respect one must have for the "image of G-d" extends beyond taking or saving a human life. Are there acts that don't involve physical harm, but which are spiritually equivalent to murder? For example, can one be guilty in the eyes of G-d for destroying another's reputation, or subjecting him to humiliation? What if the publicized damaging information is true? These questions, as well as many more, are addressed in the Noahide Code. Specifically, "Murder and Injury" covers obvious issues such as homicide (whether premeditated murder or accidental manslaughter), suicide, euthanasia, and causing serious physical injury. It covers issues such as the Torah Laws regarding permissible acts of self-defense, endangering one's life to save another, and death caused through criminal or unavoidable negligence. The prohibition of injury also extends to non-physical attacks such as slander, embarrassment, and causing emotional harm. Even though many of the precepts relating to murder and injury are complex, an underlying theme can be summarized in one sentence. It is known as Hillel's "Golden Rule" of the Torah, and it simply states, "That which is hateful to you, do not do to your fellow. The rest is the explanation; go and learn."

By extension, a person should also refrain from speaking evil about others, as well as against the Creator, for respect is due to every person by virtue of being created with a rational human soul, which is the "Divine image" within a person. If one speaks words that destroy a favorable image of a person in another's mind, then one has done actual harm, both to the person who was spoken about and to the listener. Rabbi Israel Baal Shem Tov, the founder of the Hassidic movement, explained: "Evil gossip kills all three – the inventor of the slander, the one who relates it, and the listener. This is all in spiritual terms..."

Scriptural Sources

This prohibition is stated in Genesis 9:6 – "Whoever sheds the blood of man, among man, his blood shall be shed; for in the image of G-d He made man."

Some Details and Related Principles

List of topics in the Table of Contents under the Prohibition of Murder and Injury, in "The Divine Code," Part V:

- The prohibition of murder; abortion; euthanasia; causing mortal injury, and partners in murder.

- The prohibition of suicide.

- When it is permitted to sacrifice one's life for one of the Seven Noahide Commandments.

- The laws of a pursuer and self defense.

- The laws of intentional and unintentional killing, and killing through negligence or under duress.

- The prohibition of causing personal injury or damage.

- The prohibition of endangering oneself or another.

- The obligation to save a person's life.

- The prohibitions of embarrassing another person; evil gossip, and tale-bearing.

- The laws of reproductive sterilization and contraception.

Selected rules related to the Noahide prohibition of murder and injury, from the text of "The Divine Code," Part V:

- One who injured or embarrassed another does not receive full atonement for the distress he caused just through monetary restitution alone. He should also ask forgiveness, and the person who was harmed should not be unforgiving. Rather, when he sees that the person who harmed him truly wishes to seek his forgiveness, he should pardon him.

- It is forbidden to cause another person suffering through one's speech. This is morally and logically binding, as the sage Hillel said as a summary of the *entire* Torah, "What is hateful to you, do not do to your fellow."

- One who truly repents for the sin of murder should make a complete repentance, including increasing his acts of loving kindness and his charitable giving, and providing sustenance to those who are poor and living in pitiful conditions. It is also good for him to exile himself from his place of residence and his station in life, for exile atones for the sin of murder.

4. The Prohibition of Eating Meat that was Removed from a Living Animal

The Responsibility of Human Dominion Over the Animal Kingdom

The Meaning

If meat from certain types of animals is taken for human consumption, G-d has commanded that in the process of slaughtering, it is required to wait until the animal's life has departed. Thus we see that the Creator requires us to give recognition to the animal's connection with its spiritual dimension, which is its enlivening soul. This connection departs when the heart has permanently stopped pumping blood. Torah-law teaches that this commandment applies to land mammals and birds, and by extension, that we must respect the life of all creatures by distancing ourselves from treating them cruelly. Kindness requires that we are not permitted to cause unnecessary suffering to any creature.

But we can also look deeper. This connection between the spiritual and the physical is reflected in the class of angels that have "the face of the human, the face of the lion, the face of the ox, and the face of the eagle" (Ezekiel 1:5-10). Can it be a coincidence that we are commanded to take more care when we partake of the flesh of domesticated mammals (represented by the ox), wild mammals (represented by the lion) and birds (represented by the eagle), while consumption of human flesh is always forbidden?

"There was a likeness of four angels…
each had four faces…there was a human
face, and a lion's face… and an ox's
face… and an eagle's face."

—Ezekiel 1: 5-10

The animal spirit derives from these
angels.

—Zohar III

*From the Introduction by Dr. Joe M. Regenstein, Ph.D. (Prof. of Food
Science, Cornell Univ.) to the section on the Prohibition of Meat from
a Living Animal, in "The Divine Code," Part IV:*

One of the Noahide Commandments is referred to in Hebrew as
"Eiver Min Ha'hai" ("Limb from a Living Animal"), which prohibits
eating flesh that was severed from a living animal. It is an important
statement of the limitations imposed on each individual, in light of the
broader scriptural permission for humanity to have "dominion" over
the animals. It is also a statement of G-d's concern for the welfare of
animals. Humanity's responsibility for animal welfare is further
developed in the Hebrew Scriptures to encompass the broader concept
of avoiding the infliction of unnecessary pain or suffering upon living
creatures, which is the concept of not doing any harm to animals
unless there is a good reason to do otherwise. It is thus made clear that
in G-d's judgment, to treat an animal cruelly is wrong. Therefore,
Hebrew Scripture, by showing this caring for animals, also teaches by
implication how much worse it is to treat people poorly.

Many of the modern public issues being discussed in the realm of animal welfare with respect to slaughter, pre-slaughter handling, and post-slaughter waiting for the animal to expire, are covered by the Divine Noahide Code. It is therefore a source for providing guidance to all consumers, along with the regulators and overseers of the modern meat industry, and it challenges us all to be concerned with improving the handling of animals—both on the farm and in our communities, and most importantly in the arena of the compassionate use of animals for human food. The study of the Noahide Laws can help one approach the above concerns in keeping with modern industry guidelines for animal welfare, while also meeting the ancient but continuously relevant rules of *"Eiver Min Ha'hai."*

Scriptural Sources

G-d permitted the eating of meat for the first time to Noah and his family after they left the Ark, which is why G-d at that time added the seventh commandment, which prohibits the eating of meat that was severed from a living animal (even if it was stunned and insensitive). This commandment given to Noah is recorded in Genesis 9:4. – "But flesh with its soul, [which is] its blood, you shall not eat."

Some Details and Related Principles

Adapted from the Table of Contents under the Prohibition of Meat from a Living Animal, in "The Divine Code," Part IV:

- The prohibition applies to land mammals and birds.

- The prohibition of separating meat from an animal that is living or in the process of dying.

- Consuming such meat before or after the animal's death.

- Deriving benefit from meat separated from a living animal.

- Restrictions on causing suffering to a living creature.

- The prohibition of mating different species of animals.

- The prohibition of grafting different species of fruit trees.

Selected general rules of the Noahide prohibition of meat removed from a living animal, from "The Divine Code," Part IV:

- In Genesis 9:2-3, Noah and his descendants were granted permission to kill any type of animal in any way they desired, for the purpose of food. Still, it is fitting for a person to have compassion toward animals and to kill them in the most painless manner possible. For mankind was not granted unrestricted permission to cause suffering to a living creature. Moreover, it is fitting for a person to distance himself from cruelty to the fullest extent possible.

- Noah was, however, forbidden to eat meat that was removed from certain animals while they were still living. This commandment in Genesis 9:4 refers to flesh separated from these live animals while their soul is still in their blood; i.e., while the heart is still pumping life-blood within the animal. This prohibition applies only to land mammals and to birds. These are all the animals for which there is a Torah-law distinction between their flesh and their blood.

- There are various outstanding logical explanations which can be put forth for this prohibition. For example, the obtaining of such flesh is likely to be done in a way that would result in great pain to the animal. Furthermore, it is a cruel behavior, which is a trait that people should strive to avoid. Nevertheless, it is from G-d's statement, "But flesh with its soul, [which is] its blood, you shall not eat," that we learn that any flesh that is separated in any manner from the animals that are covered by this prohibition, during the time they are alive, is forbidden to be eaten.

- After Noah left the ark, humans were granted permission to kill any animals for food, or for the use of their body parts for beneficial purposes. However, they were not granted permission to injure, kill, or cause suffering to an animal for no useful purpose, and one who does so violates the prohibition of causing unnecessary pain to a living creature. For this reason, it is forbidden to skin an animal or cut out one of its organs during its lifetime, even if one does not intend to eat from the part removed. Instead, if one requires the hide or organ, one should kill the animal first and then take the parts of its body that one needs.

5. The Prohibition of Theft

Responsibility and Respect for Ownership of Personal Property

Rabbi Yosay said: "Let the money of your fellowman be as respected by you as your own."

—Ethics of the Fathers, Ch 2.

The Meaning

From the Introduction by Rabbi Moshe Weiner to the section on the Prohibition of Theft, in "The Divine Code," Part VII:

The Prohibition of Theft and its laws are unique in that they connect to almost every aspect of life, since societal people must deal with others continuously: buying, selling, and exchanging items. The focus of this command is to accept and honor another person's needs and money. Theft in its different forms causes corruption, which can bring society to the brink of destruction. This lesson has been historically documented in the decline of many societies.

A unique point borne out from this command is that one must justly accept others as equal to oneself, honoring them and their property. This feeling can only come from the recognition that all people are equally created by the One G-d, who creates all and provides for all. As each person is allotted an exact and appropriate portion from G-d, there is no reason to desire or take that which belongs to another. Another lesson is the importance of being truthful. One must contemplate that being truthful and just is not only necessary for the upkeep of society, but is also for one's own sake and benefit. Truth is being correct with oneself, to recognize one's true virtues, capacities, needs, and duties.

No one knows each individual person's needs better than mankind's Creator Himself, Who gave us commands and a pattern of life to be successful and maximize our potential. However, a person needs a vessel to receive this pattern of life, to accept it and manage to live with it accordingly. This vessel is truth.

One must be extremely careful about theft, since there are many details. A person naturally covets the money of others, and one's evil inclination tricks him with various excuses for why it would be permissible. This law helps a person remain focused on G-d and His truth, and to remain truthful with oneself. One should also exert extra effort to learn and understand this law and its details in order not to transgress the prohibition even by mistake. It is also an obligation to guard one's actions, since one is more likely to mistakenly steal when one is not taking careful notice of his actions.

Scriptural Sources

The prohibition of theft is contained within the permission which G-d granted to Adam and Eve in Genesis 2:16 to eat from the trees of the garden. This implies that if permission had not been granted, they would have been forbidden to do so, since the property did not belong to them. This Noahide commandment is cited explicitly by Abraham in Genesis 21:25.

Some Details and Related Principles

Adapted from the Table of Contents under the Prohibition of Theft, in "The Divine Code," Part VII:

- The prohibition of (secretive) theft and (open) robbery.

- The obligation to return a stolen object, and restitution for theft.

- The prohibitions of assisting a thief or benefiting from stolen items.

- Saving a life overrides the prohibition of theft, but the amount taken should be paid back if possible; retrieving a stolen object.

- Theft through false measurements; the prohibition of cheating or misinforming another person.

- The prohibition of extortion, and forcing a purchase.

- Laws of borrowing, renting, and safeguarding an entrusted object.

- Stealing or encroaching upon real estate property.

- The prohibition of kidnapping.

- Bodily injury and damaging another person's property.

- Delinquent debts, and withholding a worker's wages.

- The laws pertaining to an ownerless object.

- Gambling and other activities that are similar to theft.

Selected rules related to the Noahide prohibition of theft, from the text of "The Divine Code," Part VII:

- In the Noahide Commandments, there is no difference between theft (stealing secretly) and robbery (stealing openly).

- Extortion occurs when one forces his victim to sell him an object, even at its correct value. This is also forbidden.

- If the item taken is so small that no one would be concerned about it (for example, a wood sliver taken from a fence for a toothpick) it is permissible. But if many people are involved and each one takes a small amount, the owner would mind, and it is forbidden.

6. The Prohibition of Forbidden Sexual Relations

Defining the Boundaries of Intimacy

"A man shall cling to his wife and they shall become one flesh."
—Genesis 2:24

"One flesh: the child is formed through the two of them, and in this way their flesh becomes one."
—Explanation by Rashi

The Meaning

One of the most powerful human desires is the desire for sexual fulfillment, which is necessary for procreation and thus the continuation of humanity. But when used destructively, it has not only destroyed the morals of individuals, but it has also been proven to lead to the disintegration of whole societies.

The Hebrew words for man *(ish)* and woman *(ishah)* both contain the Hebrew root word *aish*, fire. The Talmudic Sages drew a correlation between the words: just as fire can be harnessed to produce energy and provide great benefit, but when unleashed it can also bring destruction and ruin, so too, human sexual desire must be kept within the boundaries of a productive and G-dly marriage.

From the Introduction by Arthur Goldberg, author of "Light in the Closet," to the section on the Prohibition of Forbidden Relations, in "The Divine Code," Part VI:

The Torah places much emphasis on the value of the family and the furtherance of societies. Wholesome families are the foundation upon which healthy communities, nations, and societies are built. Without a foundation, the mightiest building is bound to crumble. As explained in the Written Torah and Talmud, a main accomplishment of the sexual prohibitions is rejection of unbridled licentiousness that leads to the disintegration of society. The modern vision of morality (which mirrors much of ancient paganism) is often rationalized as a virtually all-permissive, "anything goes" social system founded on a concept of universal "tolerance." Unfortunately, this concept of tolerance is, in actuality, a facade used to mask an agenda of sexual licentiousness.

History confirms the importance of these Torah lessons. The British anthropologist J. D. Unwin's comprehensive and classic study of 5,000 years of history chronicles the historical decline of 86 primitive and civilized societies. He found that "the regulations of the relationship between the sexes" are the very foundation of civilized society.[1] Unwin discovered (contrary to his personal philosophy and inclination as a social liberal) a distinct correlation between increasing sexual freedom and social decline.

If the authentic Torah teachings on true sexual morality are followed, humankind hopefully will not *self*-destruct. G-d provided a rainbow as evidence of His covenant that He will not destroy the world again. The seven colors of the rainbow correspond to the Seven Noahide Laws – the foundations of a G-dly and ordered society. But because G-d endowed mankind with free choice, there is the ever-present question concerning whether a society will heed them – particularly the admonitions of sexual boundaries and proscriptions. These are set forth as a code of laws involving sexuality. If Gentiles live their lives consistent with this Biblical framework of morality, then the rainbow can also represent a multi-level system of spiritual wholeness that enables them to live righteous lives and have a share in the World to Come. This then becomes the opportunity for a covenant between humans, and a basis upon which we can create a world of wholeness and holiness.

[1] J. D. Unwin, *Sex and Culture,* Oxford Univ. Press, 1934.

Scriptural Sources

Five of the six types of relations that are forbidden by G-d to Gentiles are covered in Genesis 2:24: "Therefore a man shall leave his father and his mother and cling to his wife and they shall become one flesh." This verse explicitly forbids relations with one's mother, one's father's wife, a wife of another man, another male, and an animal. A Gentile is also forbidden to have relations with his maternal sister, which is learned from Genesis 20:13: "Moreover, she is indeed my sister, my father's daughter, though not my mother's daughter; and she became my wife." (Note that Abraham said this to appease Abimelech. It was actually only figuratively true in his case, since Sarah was the daughter of Abraham's brother. They had the same paternal grandfather, whom people often referred to as "father".) It was also universally accepted that father-daughter relations would be prohibited, as evidenced by the disgrace of Lot after he had relations with his two daughters, following G-d's destruction of Sodom and Gomorrah (Genesis 19:29-36, and Rashi on Genesis 20:1). Relations between females are likewise an abomination to G-d. It is one of the subjects of Leviticus 18:3, which speaks against the immoral practices of the ancient Egyptians and Canaanites, and which Leviticus 18:30 refers to as "abominable traditions." About this the Midrash specifies: "A man would marry a man, a woman would marry a woman, and a woman would be married to two men."

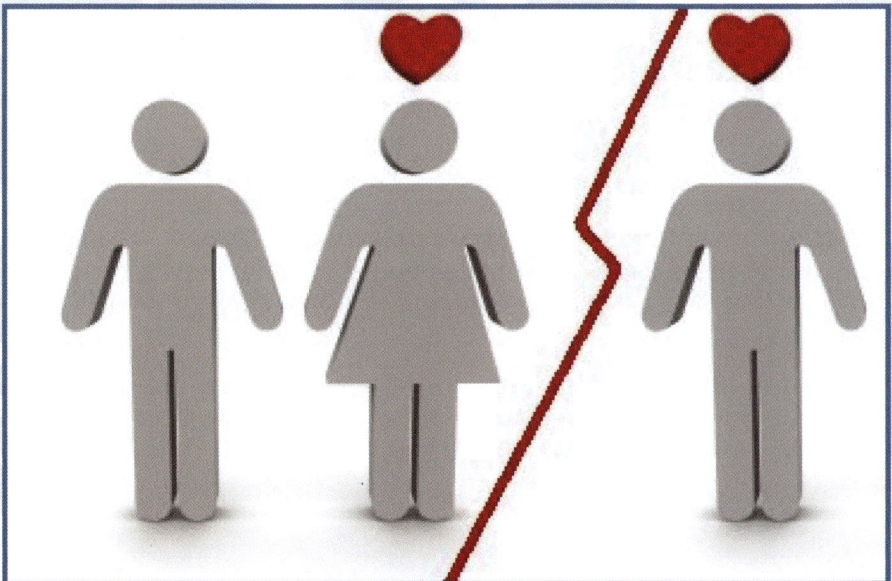

Some Details and Related Principles

Adapted from the Table of Contents of the Prohibition of Forbidden Relations, in "The Divine Code," Part VI:

- Categories of forbidden sexual partners and sexual acts.

- The prohibitions of homosexual and bestial relations.

- The prohibition of relations with other men's wives.

- Partners with whom there can be no status of marriage.

- Precepts related to marriage, fornication, and divorce.

- Precepts related to spilling semen and contraception.

- Guarding against forbidden relations, and following ways of modesty.

- Prohibitions related to being alone with a forbidden partner.

Selected rules related to the Noahide prohibition of forbidden relations, from "The Divine Code," Part VI:

- A few other sexual relations that are not capital sins are also forbidden. For example, a full sister or maternal half-sister of a man's mother is forbidden to him.
- If Gentile societies see a need to impose upon themselves extra restrictions, and enforcedly prohibit relations between other categories of relatives, they are permitted to do so. (For example, almost all societies have prohibited marriage between an uncle and his niece.)
- There is no status of true marriage for those who are minors according to Torah Law, since they do not have the maturity of mind to accept a marital bond. An even higher minimum age at which to allow and recognize marriages should be set by some communities. This should be the age when most people in that community are considered to be mature and responsible for their actions. Nowadays, this is usually in the late teens.
- G-d's words (Genesis 2:24), "Therefore a man shall leave his father and his mother and cling to his *wife,* and they shall become one flesh," reveal that it is natural and appropriate for a man to marry a woman and establish a family. One who deviates from this path acts contrary to what G-d intended for mankind.

7. The Obligation for Laws and Courts
The Foundation of a Peaceful and Just Society

The Meaning

If society is to function successfully, it must impose upon itself a legal structure to ensure adherence to core values. Peace and success among the members of a society can only be fostered if a righteous moral code is used to establish enforceable boundaries of behavior. Every nation, state or province, and municipality is obligated to have a system of courts to uphold the Noahide Commandments. Beyond this, all societies must also establish civil laws according to righteous principles, with civil courts ruling on civil matters, since these inevitably arise in daily life.

For the good of the society, courts or governments may place necessary legal limits on activities that G-d's Torah leaves up to personal choice, as long as the restrictions are acceptable to the population in general. Then by the Noahide "Law of Courts," citizens are required to observe the secular law, and the courts can apply any non-capital punishment that the public in general accepts, as long as it is not cruel or unusual. This is called "going beyond the letter" of the Torah Law. For example, a court system has the right to limit male citizens to only one legally contracted wife at a time (including both formally registered marriages and common-law marriages), if this is judged to be a benefit for the society.

Furthermore, G-d's known standards for moral human behavior are part of His desire for "yishuv olom" (literally, "settling the world," which is a Biblical term that refers to people making societies that are peaceful and proper in G-d's eyes). Therefore, establishing righteous laws and courts also falls under the Noahide obligation to promote "yishuv olom" – people should be encouraged to act in ways that are morally proper according to G-d, or at least refrain from acting in ways that are known from the Hebrew Scriptures (which are authentic Divine revelation) to be abhorrent to G-d. This applies whether or not the undesirable actions are actually liable to punishment according to the Torah's Noahide Code.

Adapted from the Introduction by Rabbi Dr. Shimon D. Cowen to the section on the Establishment of Laws and Courts, in "The Divine Code," Part VIII:

The Noahide precept of justice, or *dinim*, is the obligation, incumbent upon societies, to establish the rule of law through courts in every district of the land. It is, however, not simply the establishment of law and order specifically in reference to the Noahide Laws, which have somewhat of a parallel in secular legal philosophy that might be called an order of "natural justice." In actuality, it is the Divine template for human conduct, set out in the Hebrew Bible and its Oral tradition. This is what Rambam (Maimonides) intends when he states that the Noahide precept of establishing a system of justice is for the purpose of ruling on the other six universal Noahide Laws. That is to say, justice itself is one of the Seven Noahide Commandments, with its own parameters.

In defining the precept of *dinim*, the words of Rambam are "to judge in relation to these six [other] precepts" and this is understood to exclude judgment in certain areas where punishment is given over to the hands of Heaven instead of the courts. Still it would appear that the precept applies to three areas: (a) the actual prescriptions in the Noahide Laws as set out in the Biblical revelation to Moses at Sinai, and elucidated in the Oral tradition which also derives from Sinai; (b) an area of rules and arrangements in the realm of justice, mandated by reason for the purposes of social order; (c) a domain of adopted stringencies, whereby higher standards of justice are taken on and become part of Noahide law.

The normative legal system is thus not a mere reflection of community values or a repository of statutes given by a legislative body, but of the Noahide Code, within which community values – including legislated laws and norms – are included so long as these are consistent with the Noahide Laws. Judges, lawmakers and the enforcers of law all need to be cognizant of this higher, universal code. Where there is doubt as to the parameters of Noahide law in regard to new matters, the filling of this gap can be done only by a qualified Orthodox Rabbinic authority in the Noahide Laws.

The function of the system of justice is also put "negatively": to disallow disorder. Here Rambam writes that the function of courts under Noahide law is to "warn the people" against its infringement. This therefore presupposes a responsibility on the part of the State's agencies of justice: both of the duly instituted ruling government and the judiciary.

The precept of *dinim* is of particular contemporary importance, even in societies with high standards of impartiality and freedom from corruption in the administration of justice. This is because personal value judgments and beliefs can and do enter the rulings of judges, resulting in decisions which are at variance with the Noahide Laws. This we have seen in rulings permitting homosexual "marriage," abortion on demand and euthanasia. The judge must first and foremost know and be beholden to the universal Noahide Laws as the background ethical conditions for all positive (human-made) law and its adjudication.

Scriptural Sources

G-d commanded Noah regarding the trial and punishment of a murderer, as it says in Genesis 9:6, "Whoever sheds the blood of man, among man, his blood shall be shed…" This refers to a Noahide commandment to judge and penalize a murderer.

This is explained as follows by the Talmudic Sages: "Whoever sheds the blood of man" (referring to the murderer), "among man" (i.e., he is to be prosecuted in a court by a man who is qualified to testify as a witness), "his blood shall be shed" (if convicted, he is liable to capital punishment by the court). The Noahide Code commanded through Moses at Mount Sinai specifies that Gentiles are similarly obligated to bring transgressors of the other Noahide commandments to justice in a court of law.

Some Details and Related Principles

- The ruling power must institute oversight over the courts to be sure that only proper and expert judges are appointed, and that the judges do not act corruptly or unrighteously. The ruling power also has the authority to institute a structure of "appeals" or "referral" courts.

- Every individual must abide by a properly rendered legal decision he has received. It is forbidden for an individual to carry out judgments and punishments against others (vigilante justice). One must pursue a legal case within the legal system that has jurisdiction over the matter.

- Standard types of evidence are admissible in Noahide courts.

- Anyone who is known to transgress any of the Noahide Commandments is not to be considered as a reliable witness in capital cases.

- All judges must deliver righteous judgments, and opposing claimants must be treated equally in all ways.

- Bribing a judge is forbidden, and judges may not take bribes.

- In civil cases, one should seek arbitration, mediation or other means of finding an amicable settlement or compromise.

- If the majority of the society is not G-d fearing and does not observe all of the Seven Noahide Commandments, a court may only use capital punishment as a decree of the government to protect the society from very dangerous criminals, such as murderers.

What other righteous traditions were accepted by mankind after the Flood?

In addition to the Seven Noahide Commandments, the nations of antiquity voluntarily accepted several rules of moral behavior. Six of these meritorious activities are described in Chapter 4, "The Seven Universal Laws of Noah," in the book by David Sears, *Compassion for Humanity in the Jewish Tradition* (pub. by Jason Aronson, 1998). The following list of these righteous practices is taken from this book with the gracious permission of the author, in synopsis.

- **Contemplation of G-d:** Abraham discovered G-d by contemplat-ing the origin of the universe. Following his example, contemplating nature and searching out its mysteries can be a path to G-d. Contemplating the omnipresence of the Creator, Who is the Source of existence and the only True Existence, is another spiritual practice discussed in Kabbalistic and Hassidic works. However, for most people, it is very difficult to progress on the proper path without being guided by a Torah teacher. Unlike Abraham, we live after the Torah was given, so it is the mission of each individual to learn and observe the Divine commandments that apply to him personally.

Synopsis of excerpts from a talk by the Lubavitcher Rebbe, Rabbi Menachem M. Schneerson, on 11 Nisan 5743 (25 March 19'83): "In truth, thinking about G-d is itself a prayer. This is a *mitzvah* [in the sense of a righteous activity] that precludes idol worship, which is a prohibition contained in the seven universal Noahide Commandments. Since every *mitzvah* has the nature of leading to another *mitzvah* [Ethics of the Fathers, Chapter 4], surely this good deed will have a continuing good effect on the person. There is no doubt that if you inquire of the person about the events in his life in the following days and weeks [after he spends time thinking about G-d] you will recognize Divine Providence. When one thinks about G-d, the result is that later, when he considers doing something which is perhaps not proper and just, he will remember the 'Eye that Sees,' and this will stop him!"

- **Noahide Torah Study:** In order to live by the Universal Code, one must study its precepts. An outline is really just a starting point. The various ramifications of the Seven Noahide Commandments are discussed at length. The Sages of Israel taught that study of the Torah's precepts (including the Universal Code) should be in a spirit of humility and faith. Therefore, Gentiles who believe in the One True G-d and strive to live by the Universal Code should study the details of their seven commandments, as well as other parts of Torah literature relevant to their spiritual needs and responsibilities.

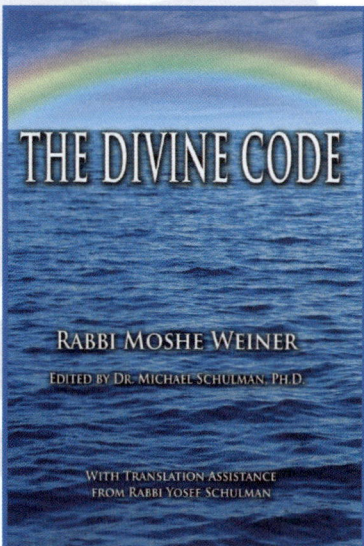

From "The Divine Code," p. 91, by Rabbi Moshe Weiner:
"Learning Torah ... [is] an obligation that is included in the Seven Commandments themselves ... the one who is commanded should know and be involved in learning how to keep that commandment. Therefore, when a Gentile learns a part of Torah for the purpose of observing a Noahide Commandment, he receives a reward, in addition to the reward for observing the Seven Noahide Commandments themselves. And even more so, since his learning Torah about the Seven Commandments is connected to the particular commandment that it relates to, the learning is a fulfillment of a directive from G-d. Therefore, learning about the Seven Noahide Commandments is called a permissible 'involvement' in Torah study, and the reward for this learning and involvement in Torah is great."

• **Prayer:** Every person can establish a relationship with G-d through prayer. One should pray to the Creator for all of his or her needs, and pray for the welfare of others. G-d receives the prayers of all who sincerely call upon Him. Thus, the Holy Temple in Jerusalem is called "a House of Prayer for all nations." (Isaiah 56:7)

Through devotional prayer one can come to experience transcendence of self and attachment to G-d. Rabbi Nachman of Breslov especially recommended going into the forests or fields in order to achieve this. (In one's home, it is beneficial to pray in a quiet, private room.) This practice is associated with Isaac, the second Patriarch, who is described as praying alone in the fields (Genesis 24:63). Isaac also prayed at home with his wife, she on one side of the room, and he on the other (Genesis 25:21).

From the book "Vedibarta Bam" (And You Shall Speak of Them), by Rabbi Moshe Bogomilsky, copyright © by Sichos In English:
What practical lesson can we learn from G-d's command to Noah to enter into the ark?... The Hebrew word *teivah* used for "ark" also means "word." G-d is telling us as well to "enter" into the words of Torah and prayer... Just as Noah was commanded to enter with his entire being into the ark (*teivah*), so are we told to "enter" with all our heart and soul into the words (*teivot*) of Torah and prayer, reading the words carefully [from a properly translated Hebrew Bible or Psalms, etc.], saying each word with feeling. In this way we will fulfill, in the spiritual sense, a previous command G-d gave to Noah: "A light shall you make for the ark (*teivah*)" (Genesis 6:16) – you shall illuminate the words ("*teivot*") of Torah and prayer with deeper feeling.

- **Good Deeds and Proper Charity:** We are all merely custodians of the wealth we possess, the purpose of which is to improve the world as much as possible. In addition to benefiting others through giving charity and other kind acts, one overcomes the ego, ceases to be a taker, and becomes a giver. Even without completely pure motives, the one who gives is meritorious, for the receiver benefits in any case... People of all nations elicit Divine mercy and protection through their acts of charity and good deeds.

- **Return to G-d:** Anyone can turn away from evil and come back to G-d at any moment, no matter what they may have done (Jonah 3:10). As the sages taught, nothing can stand in the way of repentance. The state of spiritual accord that one regains is the original unblemished condition of the soul. The prophets of Israel taught that G-d seeks the repentance of Jews and Gentiles alike (Jonah 4:11; Jeremiah 18:8). This is fundamental to the entire purpose of creation.

- **Joy:** Despair is the antithesis of faith. When one truly considers that everything is in G-d's hands and that everything is for the ultimate good, it is possible to be happy in all circumstances. Thus, the Talmud relates that a certain sage would habitually remark, "This, too, is for the good" ("*Gam zu le'tovah*"). The prophets of Israel declared that all of history is leading to a time when evil, suffering, and strife will cease. Then, all the good that mankind has accomplished will be gathered together, and G-dliness will be revealed to all. This will be in the Messianic era.

When a person realizes that by following G-d's precepts he is helping to bring the world to this state of perfection, he should be especially joyous. There is a Hassidic story that illustrates this point. Once there was a poor person who was known for his great joy. Some of his neighbors, who were having a hard time themselves, found this a bit annoying. "You're the poorest man in town," they said. "Why are you so full of joy?" "I borrowed it," he admitted, "from the better days ahead!" May we soon see the days of true joy, when at last there will be peace between nations, and "the knowledge of G-d will fill the earth like the water that covers the sea" (Isaiah 11:9).

Here are two more principles that are righteous traditions from Biblical times:

• **Honoring One's Father and Mother:** Although Gentiles were not specifically commanded about honoring parents, from the beginning of mankind's creation they distinguished themselves by accepting this as a righteous obligation.

• **Not To Deceive Others:** This is evidenced by Jacob's accusation against Laban (Genesis 29:25), "Why have you deceived me?" against which Laban took pains to *justify* himself (thus showing that he agreed that deception was considered a sin). This rule also obligated Jacob to marry Rachel, as he had originally promised her before Laban switched her for Leah, even though Jacob personally wished to restrict himself to only one wife.

Rabbi Yakov said: "This world is like an entry way before the World to Come; prepare yourself in the entry way so that you may enter the banquet hall."

He used to say: "One hour of repentance and good deeds in this world is better than all the life of the World to Come, and one hour of reward in the World to Come is better than all the life of this world."

—Ethics of the Fathers, Ch. 4

Our opportunity to all be on the same page

1. There is a single Creator of the physical and spiritual realms, Who cares about what we choose to do, and Who wants our worship to be directed to Him alone. Do not worship any other entity, whether it exists in reality or in peoples' imagination.

2. Do not curse the Creator, Whose holy Name we must revere. Let your soul feel its natural awe of Him.

3. Do not murder, for it is an attack on the image of G-d that He invested in every human being.

4. Do not eat flesh that was severed from a mammal or bird before it died. From this we learn the importance of respecting the life of all creatures, by treating them humanely.

5. Do not steal. A person who steals denies G-d's authority to allocate from His Creation to whomever He chooses. Respect the property of others.

6. Accept G-d's boundaries on human desires. Incest, adultery, homosexuality, bestiality, and other society-destroying sexual practices are forbidden.

7. Establish courts of law. A fair, effective, and consistent legal system creates a society that can receive G-d's blessings.

To learn more, ask questions, send an email, or find out how *you* can get involved, visit asknoah.org.

Printed in Dunstable, United Kingdom

64243863R00022